WITH AN AFTERWORD BY Jotaro Takagi
President of the Karate-do Shotokai

TRANSLATED BY John Teramoto

The Twenty Guiding Principles of

KARATE

THE SPIRITUAL LEGACY OF THE MASTER

Gichin Funakoshi

and Genwa Nakasone

KODANSHA INTERNATIONAL
Tokyo • New York • London

CONTENTS

INTRODUCTION John Teramoto 7

PREFACE 15

1 | 一 Do not forget that karate-do begins and ends with *rei* 17

2 | 二 There is no first strike in karate 21

3 | 三 Karate stands on the side of justice 27

4 | 四 First know yourself, then know others 31

5 | 五 Mentality over technique 35

6 | 六 The mind must be set free 41

7 | 七 Calamity springs from carelessness 47

8 | 八 Karate goes beyond the *dojo* 51

9 | 九 Karate is a lifelong pursuit 55

10 | 十 Apply the way of karate to all things. Therein lies its beauty 61

11 | 十一 Karate is like boiling water: without heat, it returns to its tepid state 65

12 | 十二 Do not think of winning. Think, rather, of not losing 69

13|十三   Make adjustments according to your opponent 75

14|十四   The outcome of a battle depends on how one handles emptiness and fullness (weakness and strength) 75

15|十五   Think of the opponent's hands and feet as swords 81

16|十六   When you step beyond your own gate, you face a million enemies 85

17|十七   *Kamae* (ready stance) is for beginners; later, one stands in *shizentai* (natural stance) 91

18|十八   Perform *kata* exactly; actual combat is another matter 101

19|十九   Do not forget the employment or withdrawal of power, the extension or contraction of the body, the swift or leisurely application of technique 105

20|廿   Be constantly mindful, diligent, and resourceful in your pursuit of the Way 109

AFTERWORD   Jotaro Takagi 116

Calligraphy by Ui Kenho
Afterword translated by Juliet Winters Carpenter

NOTE: The names of historical figures whose careers predate 1868 are
given in the traditional Japanese manner, surname preceding given name.
All other names appear in Western order.

Originally published as *Karate-do nijukkajo to sono kaishaku*
in *Karate-do taikan* in 1938.

Distributed in the United States by Kodansha America, Inc., and in
the United Kingdom and continental Europe by Kodansha Europe Ltd.

Published by Kodansha International Ltd., 17–14, Otowa 1-chome,
Bunkyo-ku, Tokyo 112–8652, and Kodansha America, Inc.

First edition, 2003
05 06 07 08 09 10 11 12   12 11 10 9 8 7 6 5 4

www.kodansha-intl.com

INTRODUCTION

These twenty principles were passed down by Master Gichin Funakoshi for the spiritual and mental development of his students. They emphasize his desire to ensure that one not be caught up in the technical aspects of karate—striking, kicking, blocking—at the expense of the spiritual side of the martial art. It is the focus on the spiritual aspects, Master Funakoshi insisted, that turns karate, the mere martial art, into karate-do, a Way.

The principles provide sustenance for practitioners at all levels of accomplishment. For the beginner, they provide an overall framework with which to approach the art. For the serious student of karate-do, they offer ongoing guidance and a chance to delve more intensely into what he or she has already learned.

A thoughtful and steady perusal of Master Funakoshi's axioms will lead us on a much deeper journey than we might initially expect. It is this aspect of the principles that makes them meaningful even to those who do not practice. Unexpectedly, technical points are forsaken for a more profound examination of the broader Way. The spotlight is shone on the mental acumen, spiritual requirements, and the larger possibilities of the training. Attitude is emphasized over stance, spirit over form.

As a result, the subtle underpinnings of these twenty principles are as applicable to our lives in general as they are to the practice of karate. They lead us to reflect on how we can better regulate our lives and treat those around us.

In short, they encourage us to "polish" not just our art but ourselves.

The principles themselves are compact, terse phrases of a profound philosophical nature. However, their very conciseness leaves them open to a variety of interpretations even in their native Japanese—some possibly quite different from the original intent.

Happily, the present work provides clarification. Funakoshi's twenty principles are accompanied by explanatory comments compiled by Genwa Nakasone, a martial arts enthusiast and contemporary of Master Funakoshi. Nakasone's text amplifies principles that were originally written as succinct guidelines to be fleshed out by oral commentary provided either in the *dojo* or in private sessions with the master or one of his disciples.

It is a pleasure to be able to present this work in English, especially since it was read and approved by Master Funakoshi. The collected thoughts provide the reader with a clearer picture of Funakoshi's true purpose and, as an aside, offer a fascinating historical and cultural window on his times.

For Funakoshi, karate practice was as much about mastering the self as the martial art. In *Karate-do Kyohan*, he wrote, "The value of the art depends on the one applying it. If its application is for a good purpose, then the art is of great value; but if it is misused, then there is no more evil or harmful art than karate."[1]

In other words, first and foremost karate is about building character. Through his principles Funakoshi sought to encourage students to pursue the deeper, more meaningful aspects of the art. The principles address issues of character and the spiritual, as well as the need for courage, honesty, perseverance, and most importantly, humility—all of which can find expression through genuine courtesy and respect.

Funakoshi was quick to caution the boastful and those who sought fame with demonstrations of outlandish physical feats.

"They are playing around in the leaves and branches of a great tree, without [having] the slightest concept of the trunk."[2] Technical skills and agility quickly pale in comparison to the importance of polishing heart, mind, and character—the very elements that define the quality of one's life.

The principles point the way to improving one's quality of life. They give guidance, both encouragement and admonishment, to the karate practitioner, while extending the boundaries toward more universal applications. The deeper truths of the martial arts are not tied to techniques, tricks, and strategies for winning—they are tied to the strategies of life.

John Teramoto

1. Gichin Funakoshi, *Karate-do Kyohan*, trans. Tsutomu Ohshima (Tokyo, New York, San Francisco: Kodansha International, 1973), p. 5.
2. Gichin Funakoshi, *Karate-do Nyumon*, trans. John Teramoto (Tokyo and New York: Kodansha International, 1988), p. 17.

PREFACE

The twenty principles of karate were established by Gichin Funakoshi as way of guiding his disciples to explore more fully the spiritual aspects of the Way of Karate, or karate-do. From ancient times, karate had been secretly taught in Master Funakoshi's Okinawan homeland. He took it upon himself to introduce and encourage the practice of karate in the capital of Tokyo, where it continues to flourish.

Those who aspire to train in the Way of Karate must not focus only on the technical aspects; they must also seek to cultivate the spiritual aspects of the Way, since true karate-do trains both mind and body. The twenty principles of Gichin Funakoshi provide those who are new to karate-do with access to the spiritual side of the martial art. For those who are already training in the art, the principles act as a rich resource for spiritual development.

The following text is comprised of short commentaries I have written on the twenty principles. Master Funakoshi has read and approved their content.

GENWA NAKASONE
1938

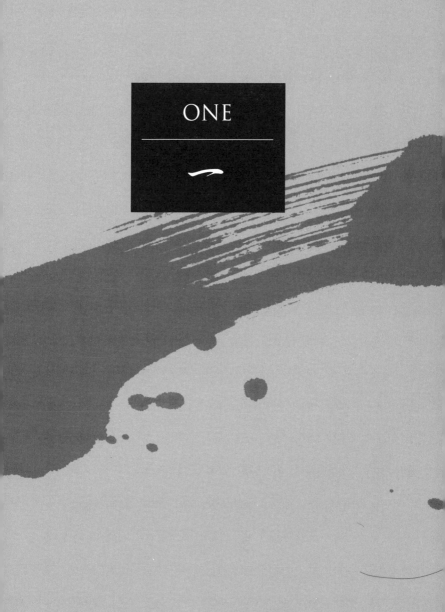

ONE

空手道は礼に始まり、礼に終る事を忘るな

1

DO NOT FORGET THAT KARATE-DO BEGINS AND ENDS WITH *REI*

Along with judo and kendo, karate-do is a representative Japanese martial art. And as with its fellow martial arts, karate-do should begin as it should end—with *rei*.

Rei is often defined as "respect," but it actually means much more. *Rei* encompasses both an attitude of respect for others and a sense of self-esteem. When those who honor themselves transfer that feeling of esteem—that is, respect—to others, their action is nothing less than an expression of *rei*.

It is said that "without *rei* there is disorder," and also that "the difference between men and animals lies in *rei*." Combat methods that lack *rei* are not martial arts but merely contemptible violence. Physical power without *rei* is no more than brute strength, and for human beings it is without value.

It should also be noted that although a person's deportment may be correct, without a sincere and reverent heart they do not possess true *rei*. True *rei* is the outward expression of a respectful heart.

All martial arts begin and end with *rei*. Unless they are practiced with a feeling of reverence and respect, they are simply forms of violence. For this reason martial arts must maintain *rei* from beginning to end.

ONE

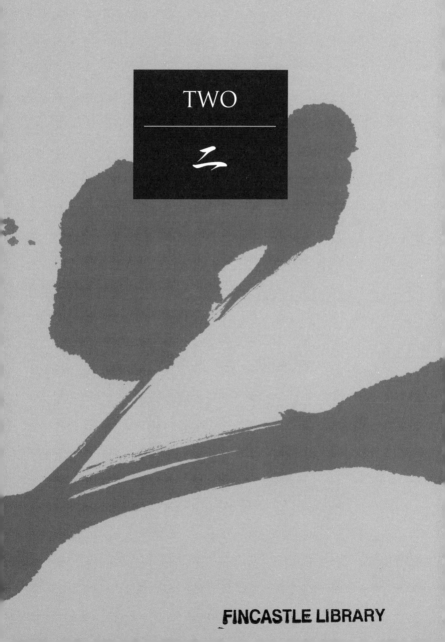

TWO

二

空手に先手なし

2

THERE IS NO FIRST STRIKE IN KARATE

"A sword must never be recklessly drawn" was the most important tenet of conduct in the daily life of a samurai. It was essential for the honorable man of the day to bear things to the very limit of his ability before taking action. Only after reaching the point where the situation could no longer be tolerated was the blade drawn from its scabbard. This was a basic teaching of Japanese *bushido* (the Way of the Warrior).

In karate, the hands and feet can be as deadly as the blade of a sword. Thus, the principle that "there is no first strike in karate" is an extension of the basic samurai principle that one must avoid the reckless use of weapons. It underscores the absolute necessity of patience and forbearance.

This principle can also be seen in the admonitions set down by karate master Yasutsune Itosu, which state:

> . . . when it becomes necessary, one should not regret laying down one's life for the sake of lord or parents, courageously sacrificing oneself for the common good. But karate [teaches that] the true meaning of this does not apply to fighting with an enemy one on one. Therefore, in the event that you are accosted by a thug or challenged by an aggressive troublemaker, you should try to avoid striking a mortal blow. You must hold as an essential principle that avoidance of injury to others with your fists and feet is your first concern.

TWO

Even in an emergency one must strive to avoid striking a fatal blow. This may be likened to the practice of hitting an attacker with the back ridge of a sword rather than with the cutting edge. It is crucial to allow an opponent time to reconsider or regret his actions.

On the other hand, when circumstances beyond control cause practitioners to have recourse to action, they must respond wholeheartedly and without concern for life or limb, allowing their martial prowess to shine to the best of their ability. This indeed is the true spirit of *budo* (the Way of Martial Arts), and it is the correct spirit behind the second principle.

Many fail to grasp the actual meaning behind the second principle and claim that all *budo* is based on the concept of striking first. Most likely they do not even realize that the character *bu* (武), "martial," is comprised of two characters that mean "to stop" (止) and "halberds," or "spears" (戈). Thus, a martial art *stops* fighting. Likewise, the character for "endurance" or "forbearance" (忍) is an ideograph derived from a blade (刃) being supported by and controlled by the mind or spirit (心).

It is only when faced with a situation so unbearable that one's ability to tolerate it (or put an end to it without confrontation) is exhausted that the sword should be drawn from its scabbard or the spear thrust at an opponent. This is the real spirit of *budo*. Nonetheless, in a worst-case scenario where combat is unavoidable, it is proper to take the initiative, attacking time and again until victory is achieved.

THREE

三

空手は義の輔け

3

KARATE STANDS
ON THE SIDE OF JUSTICE

Justice is that which is right. To bring righteousness to fruition requires true strength and ability.

Human beings are at their strongest when they believe they are right. The strength that comes from the confidence of someone who knows he or she is right is expressed by the saying, "When I examine myself and see that I am in the right, then whether I am faced by one thousand or ten thousand opponents, I must press onward." To avoid action when justice is at stake demonstrates a lack of courage.

Karate is a martial art in which the hands and feet are like swords, and it must not be used unjustly or improperly. Karate practitioners must stand on the side of justice at all times and only in situations where there is no other choice should their power find expression through the use of their hands and feet as weapons.

FOUR

四

先ず自己を知れ、而して他を知れ

4

FIRST KNOW YOURSELF, THEN KNOW OTHERS

When one knows the enemy and knows oneself, one will not be in danger in a hundred battles. When one is ignorant of the enemy yet knows oneself, chances of victory or defeat are even. When one knows neither the enemy nor oneself, each and every battle will surely be perilous.

—Sun Tzu, "Offensive Strategy," *The Art of War*

Since ancient times, this famous passage has circulated widely among those training in the martial arts. In our personal endeavors, we know our favorite techniques and our own weak points. But in fighting, not only must we be well aware of our strengths and weaknesses, we must understand those of our adversary. Then, even in a hundred confrontations, the danger is minimal. If we know ourselves but do not know our opponent, victory or defeat depends on chance. But going into battle knowing neither our opponent nor ourselves is like taking a wild stab at something, or fighting blind—and each and every engagement puts us in peril.

Karate practitioners must be completely aware of their own strengths and weaknesses, and never become dazzled or blinded by conceit or overconfidence. Then they will be able to assess calmly and carefully the strengths and weaknesses of their adversaries, and create an ideal strategy.

FIVE

五

技術より心術

5

MENTALITY OVER TECHNIQUE

One day the famous sixteenth-century swordmaster Tsuka-hara Bokuden decided to test the abilities of his children. First, he called his eldest son, Hikoshiro, into his room. As Hikoshiro nudged open the door, he noticed that it felt heavier than usual and, feeling along the top edge of the door with his hand, he found and removed a heavy wooden headrest that had been placed there, carefully replacing it after entering the room.

Bokuden then summoned his second son, Hikogoro. When the unsuspecting Hikogoro pushed open the door, the headrest fell, but he quickly caught it and placed it once again in its original resting place.

Then Bokuden called his third son, Hikoroku. When Hikoroku, who far surpassed his two older brothers in technical ability, energetically pushed open the door, the headrest fell and hit his topknot. In a reflex action, Hikoroku drew the short sword at his waist and cut the headrest in two before it hit the tatami matting on the floor.

Bokuden said to his sons, "Hikoshiro, the one who passes on our method of swordsmanship has to be you. Hikogoro, if you exert yourself and don't give up, you may someday reach the level of your brother. Hikoroku, in the future you will surely cause the ruin of this house and bring shame upon your father's name. It will not do to have someone as imprudent as you in this house." And with that he disowned Hikoroku.

This story exemplifies the principle that in martial arts mental faculties are more important than technique. The former must rise above the latter.

Another well-known story can be used to illustrate the principle of "mentality over technique." Among Bokuden's disciples there was a man of extraordinary technical skill. While walking down the street, this disciple passed a skittish horse that suddenly kicked at him, but he deftly turned his body to avoid the kick and escaped injury. Bystanders who witnessed this said, "He well deserves being called one of Bokuden's top disciples. Bokuden will surely pass his secrets on to him, if to no one else.

But when Bokuden heard of the incident he was disappointed and said, "I've misjudged him," then expelled the disciple from his school.

People could not understand Bokuden's reasoning and

decided that nothing could be done but observe how Boku-den himself would behave in similar circumstances.

In order to do this, they hitched an exceedingly ill-tempered horse to a wagon on a road along which they knew Bokuden would pass. Secretly watching him from a distance, they were surprised to see Bokuden give the horse a wide berth by crossing to the far side of the road.

They were caught off guard at this unexpected outcome, and later, confessing their ruse, they asked the reason for Bokuden's sudden dismissal of his disciple.

Bokuden replied, "A person with a mental attitude that allows him to walk carelessly by a horse without considering that it may rear up is a lost cause no matter how much he studies technique. I thought that he was a person of much better judgment, but I was mistaken."

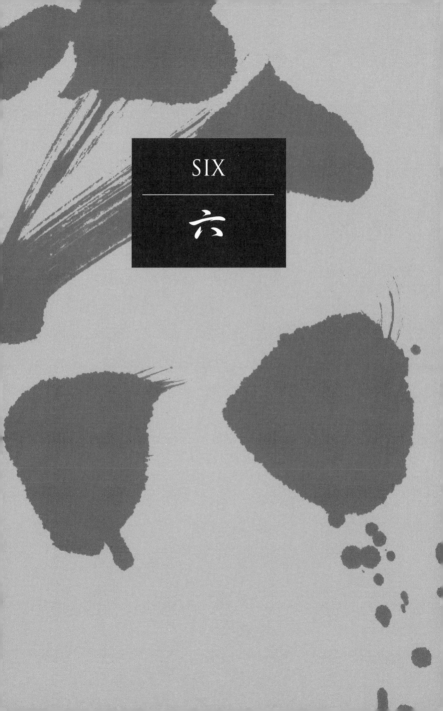

SIX

六

心は放たん事を要す

6

THE MIND MUST
BE SET FREE

It is essential to lose the mind [in order to free it].

—Shao Yung, eleventh-century Chinese philosopher

The Zen master Takuan gives his interpretation of this principle in his book *Immovable Wisdom*, in which he uses the secrets of Zen to explain the secrets of swordsmanship to swordmaster Yagyu Munenori:

There is a phrase "to search for the lost mind," but there is also a saying, "It is essential to lose [free] the mind." Confucian philosopher Meng Tzu [Mencius] speaks of searching for the "lost" mind; looking for the mind that has strayed in order to return it to oneself. Meng Tzu observes that should our dog, cat, or chickens become lost, we will go to great pains to find them and bring them back home. He rightly points out how outrageous it is, then, that when the mind—which is the master of the body—wanders down the wrong path and becomes lost, we make no attempt to find it and bring it back.

Conversely, Shao Yung argues that the mind *needs* to become lost. Shao Yung states: "If one ties down the mind, like a cat on a leash, it will lose its freedom of movement. Use the mind well, letting it go free wherever it will, neither becoming attached to nor restrained by things." Beginners often keep too tight a control over themselves. They mistrust the idea of opening their mind and letting it run free.

But our mind should be allowed to move about freely, even if it seeks muddy recesses. The lotus blossom is not sullied by the mud in which it grows. Similarly, a finely polished crystal ball left in the mud is impervious to stains.

To reign in the mind tightly takes away its freedom. To keep our mind in close confines may be a necessary beginner's habit, but doing so for our entire life prevents us from rising to a new level, and will result in a life of unfulfilled potential.

Therefore, when we are in training, it is best to follow Meng Tzu's prescription in the early stages, but later to allow the mind freedom by following the path set out by Shao Yung.

SEVEN

禍は懈怠に生ず

7

CALAMITY SPRINGS
FROM CARELESSNESS

Carelessness—a great enemy;

the flames leap higher and higher.

   —commentary on a traditional Japanese game card

This admonition can be applied to many facets of life. Ninety-nine percent of traffic accidents are due to carelessness. At work, a bit of sloppiness can undo exhaustive research and preparation, resulting in inconsistencies or an inability to obtain anticipated results. The same is true in war, whether in a battle involving armies or in individual combat. Careless preparation, or outright negligence, is a clear formula for disaster.

To prevent our efforts from "going up in flames," we should constantly examine our actions and be cautious about our methods, being ever mindful that "calamity springs from carelessness."

EIGHT

八

道場のみの空手と思うな

8

KARATE GOES BEYOND THE *DOJO*

The objective of karate-do is to polish and nurture both the mind and body. The cultivation of one's spirit and mental attitude begun during practice in the *dojo* (training hall) should not cease after the physical and mental exertions end for the day. Rather, this should continue outside the *dojo*, in our daily routine.

Conversely, the effects of immoderate eating and drinking

and other habits detrimental to one's health outside the *dojo* will soon carry over to practice in the *dojo*. They will lead to fatigue of both mind and body, making it impossible to ever realize the goal of one's training.

Whether inside or outside the *dojo*, karate practitioners must always aim to develop and train both their minds and their bodies.

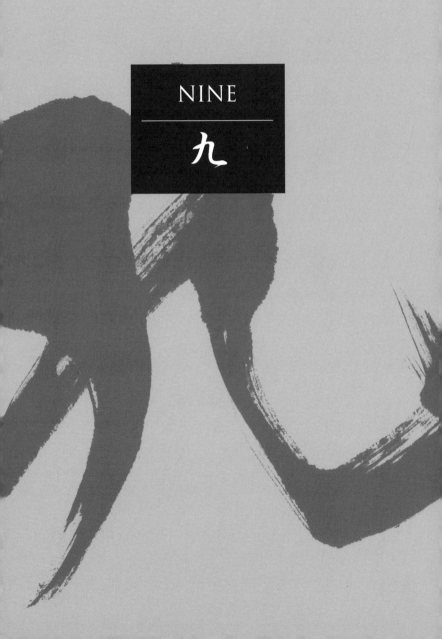

NINE

九

空手の修業は一生である

9

KARATE IS
A LIFELONG PURSUIT

There is no single point that marks the completion of karate training; there is always a higher level. For this reason practitioners should continue training throughout their life.

The true path of training is a boundless road with no end. Simply having learned all the *kata* (formal exercises) and blocking techniques does not constitute true training unless one continues to polish them. A passage in the first book of *Hagakure* supports this assertion:

In a tale of an aged swordmaster it says that there are stages to a lifetime of training. At the lowest level, even though one trains, there are no positive results and one holds oneself and others in low esteem. At this stage one can be of no service.

In the middle stage, although one still cannot be of service, one at least sees one's shortcomings and can also recognize deficiencies in others.

In the upper stage, one comes into one's own, taking pride in accomplishments, rejoicing in praise from others, and also feeling sorrow when others fail. One holds others in high esteem. For most people, this is the final stage.

But if one reaches for the next, higher step, one encounters a superior Way. If one chooses to walk this path, one finally comes to see that there really is no end. All thoughts of having come far enough vanish and one truly comes to know one's deficiencies. One lives one's life out with no desire for worldly success, one feels no need for pride, nor does one feel a need to humble oneself.

Lord Yagyu said he did not know the way to defeat others, but he knew the way to gain victory over himself—it was to become better today than yesterday, and better tomorrow than today—working in this manner day by day, all one's life.

Walking this endless road, becoming better today than yesterday, and then better tomorrow than today—throughout one's life—is a true image of the Way of Karate.

TEN

十

凡ゆるものを空手化せよ、其処に妙味あり

10

APPLY THE WAY OF KARATE TO ALL THINGS. THEREIN LIES ITS BEAUTY

One blow or one kick, given or taken, can mean life or death. This concept forms the soul of karate-do.

If all aspects of life are approached with this spirit of seriousness, all manner of challenges and hardships can be overcome.

When practitioners confront hardships with the attitude that their life is at stake, it will reveal to them what can be accomplished through their own abilities. They will come to see the wonderful power that stems from polishing the mind and body through the Way of Karate, and will recognize the exquisite beauty of this path.

ELEVEN

十一

空手は湯の如し、
絶えず熱を与えざれば
元の水に還る

11

KARATE IS LIKE BOILING WATER: WITHOUT HEAT, IT RETURNS TO ITS TEPID STATE

Learning through practice is like pushing a cart up a hill: if you slack off, it will slip backwards.

—a Japanese proverb

In all our studies, continuous concentration and diligence are the hallmark of success. It is meaningless to begin the study of karate-do as if you were stopping by a roadside stand for a refreshment on your way home. A random sampling of karate, or random practice, will not suffice. Only through continual training will you be able to obtain, in mind and body, the fruits of the Way.

TWELVE

十二

勝つ考えをもつな、負けぬ考えは必要

12

DO NOT THINK OF WINNING. THINK, RATHER, OF NOT LOSING

This twelfth principle deals with one's everyday mind; the thirteenth and fourteenth principles refer to one's mental readiness in a critical combat situation.

"Knowing only how to win and not how to lose is self-defeating" was one of the last injunctions delivered by the shogun Tokugawa Ieyasu before his death. The mental attitude that considers only winning inevitably breeds excessive optimism and causes impatience and fretfulness. Practitioners who think only of winning lose their sense of humility. They begin to ignore or disregard those around them, an attitude that can create many enemies.

The best attitude to adopt is this: Based on our true strength and unshakable conviction, we are firmly resolved in our own mind not to lose to any opponent regardless of who he may be; yet, with a mild demeanor, we try as far as possible to avoid friction with others.

Follow the saying, "When angered he can make even a ferocious beast crouch in fear, but when he smiles even little children run to him." A samurai with false courage is tough on the outside and soft on the inside; the truly courageous person is gentle on the outside and tough inside.

Karate-do has always been regarded as the martial art of gentlemen. The everyday mentality of the practitioner of karate-do should aspire to be outwardly gentle but inwardly strong.

The principle of focusing on not losing has points in common with this passage by Sun Tzu:

> A strategy in commanding troops should not depend on the enemy's not coming, but rather should rely on one's own ability to await and meet him when he does come. It should not depend on the enemy's not attacking, but should rely on our not being susceptible to attack.
> —Sun Tzu, "The Nine Variables," *The Art of War*

In short, the above passage warns us always to be prepared, an admonition that is widely applicable in many facets of our daily lives.

THIRTEEN
FOURTEEN

十四十三

戦は虚実の操縦如何にあり

敵に因って転化せよ

13

MAKE ADJUSTMENTS
ACCORDING TO
YOUR OPPONENT

14

THE OUTCOME OF A BATTLE
DEPENDS ON HOW
ONE HANDLES EMPTINESS
AND FULLNESS
(WEAKNESS AND STRENGTH)

The form of an army should imitate water. Water avoids the high and seeks the low; soldiers should avoid the enemy's fullness [strength] and attack his hollows [weakness]. Water regulates its flow depending on the shape of the terrain; an army achieves victory by responding to the enemy.

Thus it can be said that there is no standard military operation, just as there is no normal shape to water. He who gains victory by skillfully adapting to the enemy's strengths and weaknesses is called exalted.

—Sun Tzu, "Fullness and Emptiness," *The Art of War*

Principles thirteen and fourteen deal with one's mental attitude in battle.

Sun Tzu discusses the management of one's forces in relation to water. Just as water naturally flows from a higher place to a lower one, a commander hopes to avoid the enemy's strengths and to strike at his weaknesses. And just as water changes the shape of its flow according to the contours of the land—becoming slow and quiet on level land, rushing quickly down steep slopes, and cascading over the edges of cliffs—an army should adapt itself to the enemy's movements and the terrain in order to secure victory.

Therefore, in commanding and directing soldiers, a leader should avoid a "standard" military action. That is, a leader's strategy should be as fluid as water: flexible rather than fixed and unchanging. His army should move freely and skillfully and adapt to the enemy's situation. The person who can gain victory in this manner is truly superb in military strategy and timing.

As described above, one can understand the importance of chosing a strategy according to the enemy, of handling his "emptiness and fullness." This concept is not limited to the command of large numbers of soldiers but can be applied, in a narrower sense, to the technical aspects of combat in karate-do.

THIRTEEN ∎ FOURTEEN

The nineteenth principle also reinforces the importance of flexibility in one's fighting methods: "Do not forget the employment or withdrawl of power, the extension or contraction of the body, the swift or leisurely application of technique." The application of these must vary in relation to the opponent's employment of techniques.

There are many well-known proverbs that stress the necessity of adjusting one's actions to one's opponent, such as "Adapt one's speech to the audience" and "When in a village follow its customs."

The thirteenth and fourteenth principles have deep significance not only in combat and karate-do but also in the confrontations and challenges of daily life.

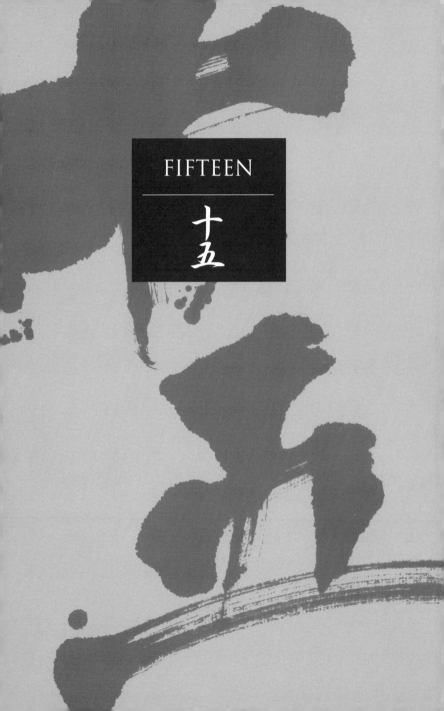

FIFTEEN

十五

人の手足を剣と思え

15

THINK OF THE OPPONENT'S HANDS AND FEET AS SWORDS

Since the hands and feet of the dedicated practitioner of karate-do can be as dangerous as a sword, this principle should be taken literally.

If we take this idea a step further, we should also consider the hands and feet of a nonpractitioner to be dangerous. When survival is at stake, even the untrained are capable of unleashing amazing power and extraordinary strength with their limbs. When someone without knowledge of karate or judo and the like fights with all his or her heart and soul and without regard for life or limb, a beginner in the martial arts would have no chance of resisting. As the saying goes, "A cornered mouse will bite even a cat."

For this reason we should never succumb to overconfidence or arrogance about our strength and ability. Whether confronted by someone with or without martial arts training, we must allow for the potential of the opponent.

When trouble occurs, we should always remain careful and respectful in words and actions and never look down upon opponents or discount their potential. Rather, we should concentrate on defending ourselves with full awareness and commitment.

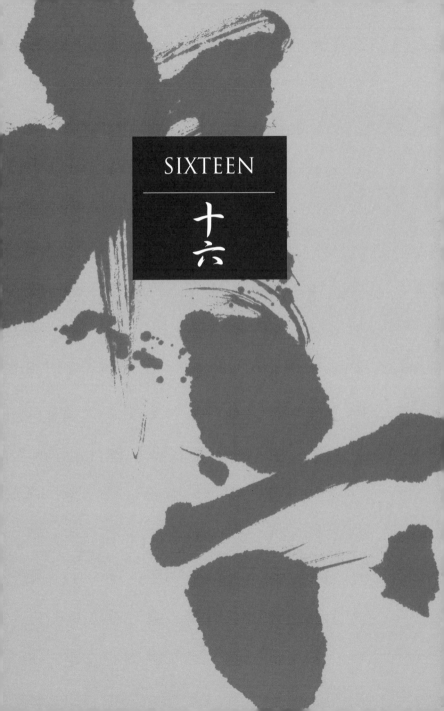

SIXTEEN

十六

男子門を出づれば
百万の敵あり

16

WHEN YOU STEP BEYOND YOUR OWN GATE, YOU FACE A MILLION ENEMIES

This principle is echoed in the ancient proverb, "When a man crosses his threshold he has seven enemies." Neither "seven" nor "a million" are to be taken literally, of course, but simply as an indication of "many."

Negligence is a great enemy when we leave the safety of our homes. If we are not in peak form in both our body and attitude, we will attract troublemakers and problems. Consequently, we should adopt the attitude that when leaving our gate we are entering into the midst of many potential enemies and should stay mentally alert.

The following story was told by karate master Kenwa Mabuni and illustrates principle sixteen:

> Master Yasutsune Itosu, a karate expert who lived a full life of eighty-five years, followed the custom of always pausing and bowing reverently before his household shrine whenever he was about to go out.

> One day, overcoming my reticence, I asked him, "Sensei, what are you requesting of the gods when you pray?"

> He replied, "When an old man like me goes out, it is thanks to the gods that I do not get kicked by a horse or run over by a carriage and that I can return home safe and sound. And so I ask them again, today, to

please protect me and allow me to finish my business and return home safely."

Still full of youthful vigor myself at the time, I said, "Sensei, what a thing for an expert martial artist like you to say!" and thought to myself that it was rather silly.

But now as I think back, I realize what a profound point of view he had.

Master Mabuni's story offers a rare glimpse into the mind of a martial arts expert and reinforces the importance of this principle.

SEVENTEEN
十七

構えは初心者に、後は自然体

17

KAMAE (READY STANCE) IS FOR BEGINNERS; LATER, ONE STANDS IN *SHIZENTAI* (NATURAL STANCE)

All forms of martial arts have their own *kamae* (postures of preparedness or readiness).

Karate has a number of *kamae* that are unique to it, and they are grounded in efficiency and effectiveness. These *kamae* have evolved from the research and experiences of karate masters of the past and have been handed down from teacher to student. When studying karate, all the *kamae* must be learned.

While still in the beginning phases, it is important to exert yourself to master the different forms of *kamae*. However, concentrating exclusively on *kamae* will inhibit the free execution of techniques, and thus the present principle has been introduced. As your training progresses it is crucial to avoid becoming attached to the concept of *kamae*. You must be able to move and change your position freely. Consider this point in tandem with that of the sixth principle, "The mind must be set free."

"Later, one stands in *shizentai*" has a counterpart in the old precept, "In karate there is no *kamae*." Since we know that karate does have *kamae*, this would appear to contradict the first half of principle seventeen, but in fact there is no conflict. Some explain this paradox thus: "In karate there is no *kamae*; but in one's *mind* there is *kamae*."

This has been said in various ways throughout the history of karate:

"Do not become distracted by overconcern with whether the physical form of your *kamae* is good or bad."

"No matter how impenetrable your ready stance may look, it is of no use if your mind is asleep."

"No matter how full of holes an opponent's *kamae* may appear, if his mind is prepared you must be extremely cautious."

In like manner, it is also a major error to become caught up in the concept of *kamae* of the mind. As an old song cautions,

It is the very mind itself
That leads the mind astray;
Of the mind,

Do not be mindless.

—Takuan Soho, *The Unfettered Mind*
(trans. Willian Scott Wilson)

In other words, we must always be on our guard against ourselves. For example, if we focus exclusively on the mental *kamae* and disregard their physical counterparts, we become susceptible. This can easily lead to carelessness and injury. "Of the mind, / Do not be mindless" points to the necessity of developing the deeper reaches of the mind—of the self—that work to suppress and quiet the deluded mind. This "inner master of the mind" is often referred to as "immovable wisdom."

All of this suggests that the idea that "in karate there is no *kamae*; but in one's mind there is *kamae*" is a waystation on the road to deeper understanding; a person's understanding is not genuine until he or she further explores the concept, attaining the realization that "in karate there is no *kamae*; in one's mind there is no *kamae*."

When practitioners reach this state of understanding, they no longer need to prepare mentally or plan for their opponent's attack or their own response. However, this state is not a blustering attitude of "Come at me with anything you've got!" Nor is it a relaxed, distanced attitude of indifference. Rather, it is an honest, open-minded composure in which the practitioner sees and responds to the manifestations of the opponent's mind and movements of the body as they emerge. The speed of the response is like the spark that results when steel strikes flint; it occurs in the twinkling of an eye, seemingly at the same instant.

This superb power is nothing less than a profound and wondrous skill. Watching a karate expert's remarkable ability to respond instantaneously will make the concept of "there is no *kamae*" crystal clear. Observing an expert will reveal the existence of an exquisite skill that manifests itself naturally according to the needs of the situation. The power of the expert with no *kamae* is echoed in this old poem that shows how, in the instant the moon appears from behind the clouds, its reflection already sits upon the water:

> Its waters never intending to reflect;
> The moon, itself never meaning to be reflected.
> The pond of Hirosawa.

How is this state of no *kamae* attained? The answer lies in the cultivation of an unperturbed mind, free of agitation. Tei Junsoku, an Okinawan scholar-sage, described the state with a similar image: "My mind, calm and clear, like water without ripples bearing a reflection." He acknowledged the importance of seeking a tranquil state of being "like water without ripples," as only then is it possible to reflect things truthfully.

Ripples on the surface of Hirosawa Pond would cause the moon's reflection to fracture into a myriad of images. Confronted with multiplicity, one grows confused and freezes, unable to move the hands or feet in a coordinated effort.

The confused mind is the cause of injury, the basis of error. It is only the constant cultivation of a composed, tranquil, immovable mind that, like a crystal clear mirror, captures the moon when it appears, or reflects a bird flying overhead. It is only the tranquil mind that can allow fair and clear judgments free of error.

"In karate there is no *kamae*"—the more one attempts to fathom the meaning of this quintessential precept of karate-do, the more one comes to appreciate the depth of its teaching. Insisting that there is no *kamae* when, in fact, all manner of *kamae* exist, follows the philosophical viewpoint that all forms of the universe are empty of real existence. The *kamae*-less *shizentai*, then, becomes a limitless number of forms.

In the depth of its content and its conciseness of expression, principle seventeen epitomizes the profound meaning of the limitless path of training that must be pursued by the karate practitioner.

EIGHTEEN

十八

形は正しく、実戦は別物

18

PERFORM *KATA* EXACTLY; ACTUAL COMBAT IS ANOTHER MATTER

Kata have been at the center of karate-do training from ancient times. Since techniques and methods of every kind have been woven into *kata*, and experts and masters from ages past have carefully preserved the various *kata*, *kata* should be practiced and performed in the same way as they are taught. In the words of karate master Yasutsune Itosu, "Keep *kata* as they are without embellishing them."

But in actual combat, it will not do to be hampered or shackled by the rituals of *kata*. Instead, the practitioner should transcend *kata*, moving freely according to the opponent's strengths and weaknesses.

NINETEEN

十九

力の強弱、体の伸縮、技の緩急を忘るな

19

DO NOT FORGET THE EMPLOYMENT OR WITHDRAWAL OF POWER, THE EXTENSION OR CONTRACTION OF THE BODY, THE SWIFT OR LEISURELY APPLICATION OF TECHNIQUE

It should be kept in mind that each of these combinations applies equally to *kata* and to actual combat. If one performs *kata* without considering the variability of power, the possibilities of the extension and contraction of the body, or the application of different rhythms when using a technique, doing them is meaningless. The hope is that through *kata*

practice and *kumite* (sparring), the practitioner should come to fully comprehend the meaning of this principle.

Employing and withdrawing power, extending and contracting the body, executing techniques quickly and slowly, inhaling and exhaling, and so on—all of these are critical elements in actual fighting and must be understood completely in order to avoid defeat.

TWENTY

女

常に思念工夫せよ

20

BE CONSTANTLY MINDFUL, DILIGENT, AND RESOURCEFUL IN YOUR PURSUIT OF THE WAY

This principle encapsulates all the principles that come before it. Whether from a spiritual or a technical standpoint, the practioner must "be constantly mindful, diligent, and resourceful."

The legendary swordmaster Miyamoto Musashi illustrates this principle:

I had my first match long ago at the youthful age of thirteen. . . . At twenty I went up to the capital, and though I met the top martial artists in the realm and fought in numerous matches, I never failed to win. After that I traveled from place to place, province to province, seeking out martial artists from various schools, and though I fought in as many as sixty duels, not once did I lose, and in that manner passed from the age of thirteen to the age of twenty-nine.

After reaching the age of thirty I thought back and saw that I won not because I was a superior martial artist. Perhaps it was because of some natural talent in this pursuit or because I did not deviate from the natural principles. Or it may have been due to inadequacies in the martial arts of other schools.

From that time I practiced fervently morning and night, seeking to grasp the principles of the Way more deeply, and around the age of fifty I came to a natural realization of the Way of Martial Arts.

—*The Book of Five Rings*

Even for a martial arts genius like Musashi, who practiced ardently morning and night without rest, it was only around the age of fifty that he first gained enlightenment of the Way.

The founder of the Muto-ryu sword style, Yamaoka Tesshu, was forty-five when he said, "I have just now attained a wondrous understanding," expressing his breakthrough to enlightenment. That was the thirty-seventh year of his training with the sword, and his twenty-third year as a disciple of the famous swordsman Asari Matashichiro. Only after continuing his practice for decades with a courageous and intrepid spirit that earned him the nickname of "Iron Demon," and only after pressing toward his goal with a seriousness of purpose that penetrated his very core, was he able to grasp the true principles of the Way for the first time.

These examples emphasize how conceited it is to indulge in the idea that it is possible to become a master of a martial art after five or ten years of leisurely practice. Such behavior misleads the practitioner and poisons the Way. This is why the final principle cautions us to "be constantly mindful, diligent, and resourceful."

Conceit or laziness are chains that impede our advancement. Karate practitioners must constantly examine and chide themselves, never failing to be mindful and diligent, until they can penetrate the innermost levels of karate-do. This must be the attitude of all who aspire to the Way.

In these few pages, I have commented briefly on the twenty principles. These principles should not be thought of as applying only to karate-do. If they and their overriding concepts of mindfulness, diligence, and resourcefulness are applied to your dealings in society as a whole, your understanding of life in general will be greatly increased.

AFTERWORD

The twenty principles in this book apply not only to karate but to martial arts across the board, and to the whole of human life. Many students of karate are under the impression that karate is first and last a tool for winning engagements and increasing your strength. But, as explained in this book, such views reflect a complete misunderstanding of the martial art. Karate is much more than simply a technique for gaining victory in combat. It is a way of cultivating the spirit. The principles here may be applied in daily life by practitioners and nonpractitioners alike.

Master Gichin Funakoshi (1868–1957) was the father of modern karate-do. As the head of Okinawa Shobukai, a karate association, he was invited to Tokyo in May 1922 by the Ministry of Education to participate in a government-sponsored exhibition of traditional martial arts. He thus became the first person ever to demonstrate the unique Okinawan (Ryukyuan) discipline of *karate-jutsu* on mainland Japan. Encouraged by men like "the father of judo," Jigoro Kano (1860–1938), and master swordsman Hakudo Nakayama (1873–1958), he stayed on in Tokyo and worked to popularize the martial art.

While giving instruction at universities, Tokyo police headquarters, and other venues, doing all he could to spread awareness of this previously unknown martial art, Funakoshi studied Zen at Engaku-ji temple in Kamakura under Chief Abbot Ekun. Around 1929, on completion of his training, Master Funakoshi bestowed a new name on the discipline then known in Okinawa as simply *te* (hand) or *tode* (Chinese hand). Funakoshi replaced the character for "Chinese," which is pronounced *kara* in Japanese, with a homonym meaning "empty." Instead of *karate-jutsu*, "Chinese-hand technique," the art became known as *karate-do*, or "the Way of the Empty Hand."

The choice of the word "empty" reflects a fundamental aspect of karate-do, which is to defend oneself and block an enemy using nothing but the unarmed hands. At the same time, the concept of emptiness echoes the Buddhist precept *shiki soku ze ku, ku soku ze shiki*, which means "the form of the universe is emptiness, emptiness is form" (see Funakoshi's autobiography, *Karate-do: My Way of Life*). The essence of Buddhism is said to be contained in the *Heart Sutra*, translated by the Chinese monk Hsüan-tsang (602–64), whose pilgrimage to India inspired the celebrated Chinese novel known in English as *Monkey*. The equation of emptiness and form is central to the teaching of the *Heart Sutra*, and Funakoshi saw striking parallels between Buddhism and his treasured karate.

As the possession of weapons was prohibited in Okinawa, the traditional discipline of *karate-jutsu* developed secretly among warriors both as a means of self-defense and as a potentially lethal weapon. When the martial art was renamed karate-do, the traditional forms took on a second purpose. They became a way of cultivating the spirit. *The Twenty Guiding Principles of Karate* was completed several years after the martial art was renamed, and aimed to provide spiritual guidance for students of karate. Simply put, the principles were intended as life lessons for those undergoing the spiritual training of karate-do.

In January 1939, the first Japanese *dojo* for the practice of karate-do was established in the Zoshigaya neighborhood of Mejiro, Tokyo. It was called the Japan Karate-do Shotokan.

Shoto, literally "wavelike sound of pines," was taken from the literary name of Master Funakoshi, who loved nothing better than to walk among the pines of his native Okinawa and listen to their branches rustling in the wind.

The first of the twenty principles is, "Do not forget that karate-do begins and ends with *rei*." On one level this means that every lesson ought to begin and end with a bow, which is called *rei*. However, on a deeper level it suggests that the karate practitioner must sincerely follow all the proprieties of karate-do—showing respect, carrying him- or herself with the proper comportment, and so on—which are also encompassed within the term *rei*. Even away from the *dojo*, the practitioner should greet acquaintances with sincere courtesy and base every aspect of his or her life on the fundamental concept of respect. The longer one continues the study of karate, the more naturally one will equate karate with propriety and respect.

As a university student, I joined a Shotokan karate club under the direction of Master Funakoshi, where I was strictly taught that fighting of any kind was forbidden. No matter what the circumstances, anyone caught fighting would be instantly expelled. Whether you were winning or losing the fight was beside the point. Master Funakoshi was adamant that anyone who misused karate techniques for fighting was guilty of cruelty. He called fighting *jaken*, which literally means "evil fists." The desire to fight turns ordinary fists into instruments of evil.

The most famous of the twenty principles is the second, "There is no first strike in karate." This principle can be interpreted as meaning that karate begins with defense, rather than a call to remain passive. Master Funakoshi wrote, "Never in any circumstance should you be the first to attack, but your mental attitude must constantly be one of seizing the initiative [should you need to defend yourself]."

At a deeper level, this principle means that in karate-do there is no self and no opponent. The practitioner of karate expands his perspective to incorporate a potential opponent and rids himself or herself of the idea of separation. This is another way in which the Buddhist precept *shiki soku ze ku, ku soku ze shiki* from the *Heart Sutra* translates into karate.

The twelfth principle declares, "Do not think of winning. Think, rather, of not losing." This means that while the practitioner should not become obsessed with the desire to win, it is essential that he or she is convinced they are not going to lose, either. The karate practitioner should not overcome his or her opponent in a frenzy to win, but should be so well trained in the art that loss is prevented.

⁓

When a celebration of the tenth anniversary of the karate club was held in the college auditorium not long after my graduation, Master Funakoshi, already in his eighties, showed up at the venue wearing his usual *hoba*, clogs with special magnolia wood supports to strengthen the legs and loins. He proceeded to give a serene and relaxed demonstration of karate. When it was all over, he summoned me. As we were talking he told me, "When you come to a bend in the road, make a wide turn. You should do this because you never know what might be lurking around the corner."

From someone at the pinnacle of his art, with such unfailing strength even in old age, it seemed surprisingly routine advice. But of all the things he told me, it made the deepest impression. No doubt the advice came, in part, from his experience in Okinawa, where the roads would then have been unlit, with no way of telling what dangers might lie hidden in the dark. To me his words conveyed the constant mental alertness of a karate master who has the foresight to circumvent danger without striking a blow. The advice Master Funakoshi gave me reflects the teachings of the sixteenth principle: "When you step beyond your own gate, you face a million enemies."

———

The eighteenth principle advises, "Perform *kata* exactly; actual combat is another matter." *Kata* have several purposes—seen and unseen. When judging tests for promotion from one level to the next, Master Funakoshi would never pass anyone who was guilty of even the tiniest error in form. "Mistakes are unacceptable," he would insist, deaf to the argument that a candidate's overall ability might be high despite his mistakes.

My own karate career now spans nearly six decades. All this time I have untiringly repeated the same training over and over, and recently I have been making all kinds of discoveries. Many things are concealed in the forms of karate—they hold lessons that no one can teach. But through sheer repetition of *kata*, it is possible to reach a point of discovery that will lead you to think, "Ah, this is it! This is what it's all about!" Beneath the surface forms of karate-do lies a deeper level of understanding accessible only to those who have mastered the necessary skills.

In a similar vein, the deepest mysteries of Japanese martial arts are recorded in secret scrolls that have been handed down through the centuries. The words and pictures of the scrolls convey nothing at all to the ordinary person. It is only after someone has devoted years of his or her life to earnest practice of the art that the mysteries of the art are revealed.

In his book *Karate-do Kyohan: The Master Text*, Master Funakoshi wrote that "karate is the foundation of all the martial arts." Certainly, a strong case can be made for this: place a sword in a karate practitioner's empty hand and you have the art of *ken-jutsu*; a stick and you have the art of *bo-jutsu*; a spear and you have the art of *so-jutsu*. The strong relationship between karate and other martial arts is evident through people such as Master Funakoshi's own teacher, Yasutsune Azato (1828–1906), who was a master swordsman of the Jigen-ryu school and was skilled in many martial arts; and the founder of the Goju-ryu school of karate, Chojun Miyagi (1888–1953), who was also reportedly an expert swordsman.

Further, the fifteenth principle reminds the karate practitioner to "Think of the opponent's hands and feet as swords." This was often quoted by Azato, a man so skilled in karate that it was said he could cut someone by simply touching them.

It is important to remember that the feet and hands can be as effective in a fight as a sword. Indeed, the Yagyu Shinkage-ryu school of *ken-jutsu* features a celebrated technique called "taking the sword," in which the practitioner captures an opponent's sword or subdues an armed attacker using only his or her bare hands. This school was founded in the Edo period (1600–1868) and was passed down by successive shoguns. Munenori Yagyu (1571–1646), the founder of the Edo Yagyu, wrote a famous book called *Heiho Kadensho*, or "The Life-Giving Sword."

According to Shigeru Egami (1912–81), one of Funakoshi's ablest students, the master was fond of saying, "Don't go against nature." This concept is encompassed within the seventeenth principle which states, "*Kamae* (ready stance) is for beginners; later, one stands in *shizentai* (natural stance)." The meaning of "natural stance" here is not easy to grasp, but basically it means that the practitioner who is no longer a beginner must maintain an ordinary demeanor. The spirit is on guard, not the body. Because there is no telling what may happen next, the spirit is fully alert, but the *kata*, or form, is relaxed.

The same idea is taught in the Yagyu Shinkage-ryu school. Without any overt sign of a ready stance, the practitioner waits for the opponent to make his or her move, and the moment the opponent attacks, the practitioner swiftly takes one step back to dodge the thrust, then strikes with the left hand forward, taking the opponent down with a single stroke. This is the quintessence of Yagyu Shinkage-ryu teaching.

The thirteenth principle advises, "Make adjustments according to your opponent," and the twentieth states, "Be constantly mindful, diligent, and resourceful in your pursuit of the Way." Besides being welcome companions to the seventeenth principle, these two guidelines bring to mind Master Funakoshi's third son, Gigo Funakoshi (1906–45), who was an ardent teacher; we looked up to him as the "young master." He was devoted to studying karate, and it was he who invented the prototype of the now-common *kata* of *mawashi-geri* (roundhouse kick) and *yoko-geri* (side kick). He also created *taikyoku no kata*, or "*kata* of the beginning of the universe," and *ten no kata*, or "*kata* of the heavens," as well as the *matsukaze kata*, "pine wind *kata*" in *bo-jutsu*. Gigo Funakoshi was engaged in a lifetime search for new styles of karate to employ so that he could adjust his own karate to that of an opponent.

———

The eleventh principle states, "Karate is like boiling water: without heat, it returns to its tepid state." In other words, practice constantly. Many people practice enthusiastically while in college, only to become distracted once they take a job, and they end up drifting away from karate. In my own life, there were a number of years when the pressure of work kept me from practicing. I regret my inattention to karate now. Looking back, it seems to me that I should have been more rigorous in my pursuit of karate, and set aside at least some time for practice no matter how busy I was. The reward comes with time and repetition. That's why I now tell people who are in the prime of their lives that, as hard as it may be, they must find time to practice. Even a few minutes a day is enough. As long as you are determined persevere with karate, you can work out a way to practice wherever you are.

———

Master Funakoshi used to say, "Karate is a path for spiritual cultivation, a physical regimen that requires no great stamina, a fitness program, and an art of self-defense." It is true that karate is not the sole preserve of those blessed with superlative strength or stamina. True karate-do is available to, and necessary for, all sorts of people around the world, of any age. And just because it is a path for spiritual cultivation, that certainly does not mean its practitioners must become overly religious or solemn. Master Funakoshi himself was a very free and easygoing person. Were he alive today, he would no doubt recommend that "every karate trainee, however busy at work or at school, [should] maintain the spirit of karate to the greatest extent possible, in as natural and relaxed a way as possible, and for as long as possible." As the ninth principle states, "Karate is a lifelong pursuit."

Jotaro Takagi
President of the Japan Karate-do Shotokai
and Principal of the Shotokan

（英文版）空手道二十訓
The Twenty Guiding Principles of Karate

2003年9月　第1刷発行
2005年7月　第4刷発行

著　者　　船越義珍

発行者　　富田　充

発行所　　講談社インターナショナル株式会社
　　　　　〒112-8652　東京都文京区音羽 1-17-14
　　　　　電話　03-3944-6493（編集部）
　　　　　　　　03-3944-6492（営業部・業務部）
　　　　　ホームページ　www.kodansha-intl.com

印刷・製本所　　大日本印刷株式会社

© 日本空手道松濤会 2003
Printed in Japan
ISBN 4-7700-2796-6